TEXAS

HISTORY TIMELINE

FROM INDIANS TO ASTRONAUTS

WRITTEN AND ILLUSTRATED BY
BETSY WARREN

STUDENT WORKSHEETS BY
PEGGY KIGER
AND
CATHY BURDITT

Hendrick-Long Publishing Company
P.O. Box 25123 • Dallas, Texas 75225

txr

ISBN- 1-885777-13-2

©1996 Hendrick-Long Publishing Company • P.O. Box 25123 • Dallas, Texas 75225

CONTENTS

INDIANS...the First Texans

It is believed that roaming tribes of people came from Asia to the American continents more that 20,000 years ago. Some of them stayed on the land which is now called TEXAS. They are known as INDIANS.

1

#1. Indians...the First Texans

Name_____

_____Date_____

_____

Questions:

1. Tell how many years ago the Indian tribes came from Asia.

_____

_____

_____

_____

_____

_____

Activities:

1. Using your dictionary, choose the meaning that pertains to the American Indians. Write this meaning._____

_____

_____

_____

2. Write a complete sentence using your own words with Indians as the subject. _____

_____

_____

_____

3. Write about a day in the life of the Indians on their journey to Texas. _____

_____

_____

_____

_____

_____

_____

_____

4. Color the worksheet.

1519... Spain

SPAIN 1519-1821

A Spaniard, Alonzo Piñeda, brought men and 4 ships to Texas shores in 1519. Piñeda claimed all the land for Spain.

Piñeda's route

#2. 1519...Spain

Name_____
_____Date_____
_____

Questions:

1. Who was the Spaniard who claimed all the land for Spain?

_____

2. How many years ago did the Spaniards first come to Texas?
_____

3. What are the symbols on the Spanish flag? _____
_____
_____
_____
_____

Activities:

1. If you were Piñeda, what names would you choose for the ships?

_____
_____
_____
_____

2. Compare the ships that sail today with ships that sailed in Piñeda's
time. _____
_____
_____
_____
_____
_____
_____
_____

3. Color the worksheet.

1528 ...Shipwrecked

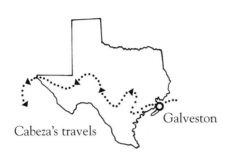

Cabeza's travels   Galveston

SPAIN 1519-1821

A group of Spaniards were shipwrecked on Galveston Island. Rescued by Indians, Cabeza de Vaca and 3 other survivors wandered with various tribes for 8 years across what is now Texas and New Mexico. Going toward the southwest, they reached Spanish-held New Mexico. Then, Cabeza sailed back to Spain and told the king what he had seen. He also wrote the first book about the land and people of Texas.

#3. <u>1528...Shipwrecked</u>

Name_____

_____Date_____

Questions:

1. What happened to Cabeza de Vaca that caused him to be with the Indians for 8 years? _____
_____
_____
_____

2. What does Cabeza de Vaca mean in English?_____
_____

Activities:
1. Locate Galveston on the Texas map shown on your worksheet. Color in the circle.
2. Trace Cabeza de Vaca's travels on your map. Name one present-day city along this route. Which direction was he traveling in Texas? _____
_____
_____
_____
_____

3. Imagine that you were with Cabeza de Vaca on his trip. Write a description about a day with him (what you saw, did, and ate).
_____
_____
_____
_____
_____
_____
_____
_____
_____
_____
_____

4. Color the worksheet.

1540...Explorers

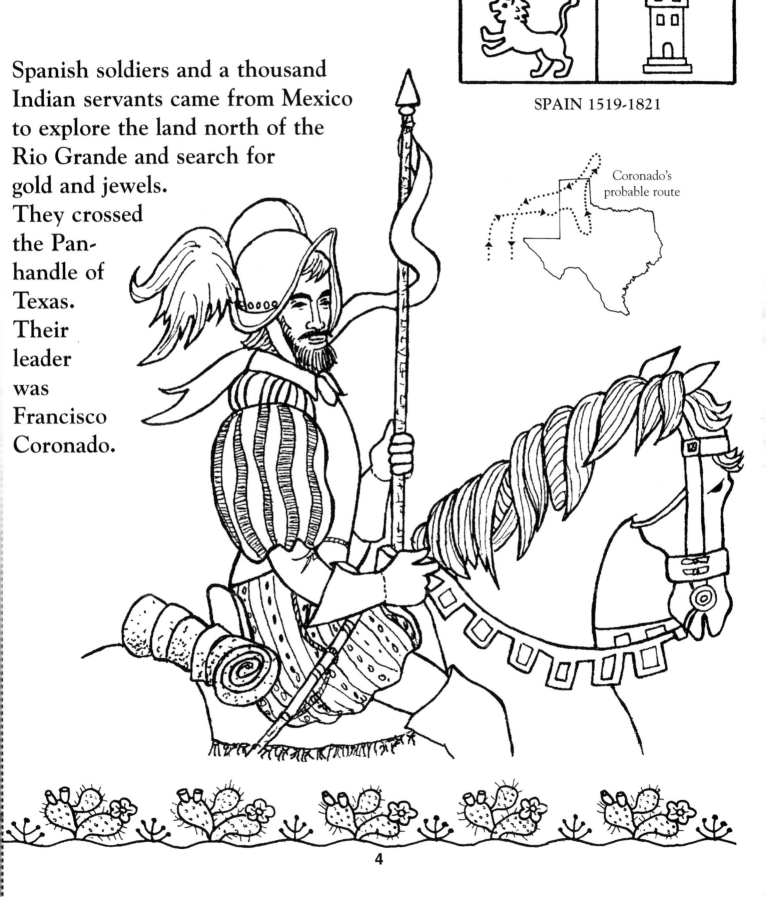

SPAIN 1519-1821

Spanish soldiers and a thousand Indian servants came from Mexico to explore the land north of the Rio Grande and search for gold and jewels. They crossed the Pan-handle of Texas. Their leader was Francisco Coronado.

Coronado's probable route

#4. 1540..Explorers

Name_____
_____Date_____
_____

Questions:

1. Give the reason Coronado came to Texas._____
_____
_____

2. Where in Texas did Coronado explore? What present-day city is located near where he explored?_____
_____
_____
_____

Activities:

1. Label the Rio Grande on your worksheet map.

2. Label your worksheet map with North, South, East and West. Circle the Panhandle area of Texas.

3. Color your worksheet.

1682...Missions

Spanish priests came into Texas to build missions. The first one was Mission Ysleta near present-day El Paso. The priests hoped to bring the Indians into the missions to teach them to be farmers and Christians who would be good citizens of Spain. The Mission Period lasted only 100 years.

SPAIN 1519-1821

#5. 1682...Missions

Name_____
_____Date_____
_____

Questions:

1. Give two reasons the priests brought Indians into the missions.

_____
_____
_____
_____

2. Where was the first mission located?_____
_____

3. Name another mission in Texas. _____
_____

Activities:

1. Name two ways you can be a good citizen. _____
_____
_____
_____
_____
_____
_____

2. Name two ways the mission on your worksheet looks like a church.
_____
_____
_____
_____
_____
_____
_____

3. Color your worksheet.

1685...
French Explorers

FRANCE 1685

The country of France sent Robert LaSalle with 200 men, women, and children to start a colony in Texas. They put up the French flag on the fort which they built near the Gulf coast. But the colony did not succeed.

Fort

#6. <u>1685...French Explorers</u>

Name _____
_____ Date _____
_____

Questions:

1. How many people did LaSalle bring to start his colony in Texas?
_____
_____

2. Give 3 reasons why you think this colony did not succeed. _____
_____
_____
_____

3. Which explorer would you rather be– Spanish or French? Give two
reasons for your answer. _____
_____
_____
_____
_____
_____

Activities:

1. The French flag shows three fleur de lis. What is a fleur de lis?
_____
_____

2. What articles of clothing are Coronado and LaSalle wearing that
are the same? _____
_____
_____
_____

3. Name at least one thing that is different that each man has. _____
_____
_____
_____

4. Color your worksheet.

1718...
the First Towns

SPAIN 1519-1821

When Spanish priests built missions in Texas, towns grew up nearby. The first town, San Antonio, grew around the Alamo mission in 1718. Goliad became a town near Mission La Bahia in 1749. The town of Laredo began in 1755.

Governor's Palace
San Antonio 1718

Mission La Bahia
Goliad- 1749

Laredo- 1755

#7. <u>1718...the First Towns</u>

Name _____

Date_____

Questions:

1. How many years are between the building of the Ysleta mission near El Paso and the building of the Alamo mission near San Antonio? _____

_____

2. Why do you think towns grew where the missions were built?

_____
_____
_____
_____
_____

3.   a) By looking at the pictures on your worksheet, of what materials are the missions made? _____

_____
_____

   b) Why were these materials used? _____

_____
_____

4. Why do you think the Spanish priests built the missions? _____

_____
_____
_____
_____
_____
_____
_____

Activities:

1. Design a mission of your own.

2. Color your worksheet.

1819....
Filibusters

SPAIN 1519-1821

Filibusters were men who fought to free Texas from the rule of Spain. With a small army, Dr. James Long of Louisiana hoped to capture Texas and give it to the United States. While he was gone for a year to gather more soldiers, his wife, Jane, waited for him on the Gulf coast. She lived in a tent with her servant, Kian, and her two little girls. Jane Long is known as the "Mother of Texas."

#8. <u>1819...Filibusters</u>

Name _____

_____Date_____

_____

Questions:

1. Give a reason Jane Long is known as the "Mother of Texas."_____

_____

_____

_____

_____

2. What does it look like Jane Long is doing in the picture? _____

_____

_____

_____

_____

Activities:

1. Describe a day in the life of Jane Long. (What did she do for food; where did she get her clothes?) _____

_____

_____

_____

_____

_____

_____

_____

_____

_____

_____

_____

_____

_____

_____

2. Color your worksheet.

1820...
Land Grants

SPAIN 1519-1821

Spain offered many acres of free land to any-
one who would come to make homes in Texas.
In Missouri, MOSES AUSTIN arranged for
300 families to come to Texas.

His son, STEPHEN, brought more
families to build homes and towns on
land granted by Spain.

#9. 1820...Land Grants

Questions:

1. What is a land grant?_____
_____
_____
_____
_____

2. How many families did Moses Austin arrange to bring to Texas?____
_____

3. What reason can you give for Stephen Austin coming to Texas
   instead of his father, Moses Austin?_____
_____
_____
_____

Activities:

1. If you were a child of a family moving to Texas, what would you
bring with you? _____
_____
_____
_____
_____
_____
_____
_____
_____

2. Look at a United States map and locate the state of Missouri,
   where the Austins began their journey. Which direction is Texas
   from Missouri?_____
_____

3. Color your worksheet.

1821...
Mexico

MEXICO 1821-1836

Mexico won freedom from Spanish rule and formed its own country in 1821. So, Texas was a part of Mexico for the next 15 years. During this time, more Spanish, Anglo and European colonists came to live in Texas.

#10. <u>1821...Mexico</u>

Name _____

_____Date_____

_____

Questions:

1. What does "freedom from Spanish rule" mean?_____

_____

_____

_____

2. How many years was Texas a part of Mexico?_____

_____

3. On your worksheet, what do you suppose is in the boy's sack?

_____

_____

_____

Activities:

1. Make your own timeline with events from the years 1519-1821.

2. Color your worksheet.

1836...
the Republic

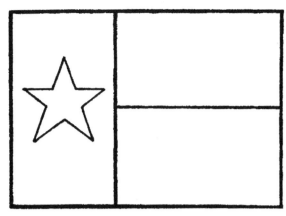

REPUBLIC OF TEXAS 1836-1846

Texans fought against the rule of Mexico in 1836. After battles at Goliad, San Antonio, and San Jacinto, the Texans won their freedom and became a REPUBLIC. Sam Houston was elected as the first president of the Republic of Texas. Stephen F. Austin was the secretary of state.

#11. <u>1836...The Republic</u>

Questions:

1. When and where did Texas become independent? _____
_____
_____
_____

2. Using your dictionary, write the meaning of "republic."_____
_____
_____
_____

3. Who do you think the man on the horse is in the picture?_____
_____
_____
_____

Activities:

1. Describe the flag of Texas. Tell what the colors mean. _____
_____
_____
_____

2. If Texas had not won its independence from Mexico, how would the history of Texas be different? _____
_____
_____
_____
_____
_____
_____

3. Color your worksheet.

1836... Capitals

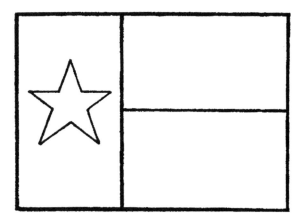

REPUBLIC OF TEXAS 1836-1846

People in the Republic formed a government that made its own laws and elected its lawmakers. The first capital was the town of Columbia. It was soon moved to Waterloo on the banks of the Colorado River. The name was changed to AUSTIN in honor of Moses and Stephen Austin.

1836
The First Capital
Columbia

1840
Waterloo
Renamed AUSTIN

Name _____

_____Date_____

_____

Questions:

1. Why was the name of the city of Waterloo changed to the name of Austin? _____

_____

_____

2. When was the first capitol building built in Austin? _____

_____

3. What's the difference in the meanings of capital and capitol? (You may use your dictionary). _____

_____

_____

_____

_____

_____

_____

_____

_____

_____

_____

Activities:

1. Locate the towns of Columbia and Waterloo on a Texas map.

2. Locate the Colorado River on a Texas map. Trace this river with your pencil to show where it begins and ends.

3. Color your worksheet.

1846...
United States

UNITED STATES OF AMERICA
1846-1861; 1865

The fine rivers and land of Texas attracted thousands of settlers from the United States as well as from foreign countries. After 10 years as a republic, Texas was admitted to the United States as the 28th state.

Oak leaves: Strength   *Olive leaves: Peace*

#13. <u>1846...United States</u>

Name _____
_____Date_____
_____

Questions:

1. What are the symbols on the Texas seal? What do they stand for?

_____
_____
_____
_____

2. How many years was Texas a republic? _____

_____

3. How many states were admitted to the United States before Texas?

_____
_____
_____

Activities:

1. Name the three rivers that form the borders of Texas.

_____
_____

2. Design your own seal for Texas.

3. Color your worksheet.

1850s...
Texas Grows

UNITED STATES OF AMERICA
1846-1861; 1865

Farmers, ranchers, merchants, shopkeepers, and their families worked hard and prospered in their businesses. Towns and cities grew larger and larger. The first trains ran in East Texas in 1853. In the same year, the governor's mansion was built in Austin.

Governor's Mansion

#14 <u>1850s...Texas Grows</u>

Name _____

_____Date_____

_____

Questions:

1. If you were one of the early settlers in Texas, what kind of job would you want to have? Give three reasons why you would pick this job. _____

_____

_____

_____

_____

2. Give two reasons why you think the towns and cities of Texas grew larger? Name the largest city in Texas now. _____

_____

_____

_____

_____

_____

3. What two important things happened in Texas in 1853? _____

_____

_____

Activities:

1. If you were traveling by train to Texas in 1853, how was traveling different from modern-day travel?_____

_____

_____

_____

_____

2. Name four ways trains in the 1850s were different from the modern-day trains. _____

_____

_____

_____

3. Color your worksheet.

1860...
Cattle Drives

UNITED STATES OF AMERICA
1846-1861; 1865

Wild horses and longhorn cattle were plentiful in Texas. Since meat was scarce in northern and western states, COWBOYS drove thousands of cattle to sell to city markets and military forts outside of Texas. When train lines were extended across the country, cattle were shipped by rail in the United States. After 20 years, there was no need for long cattle drives.

#15. <u>1860...Cattle Drives</u>

Name _____
_____Date_____
_____

Questions:

1. Why were the cowboys important to the cattle drives? _____
_____
_____
_____

2. How did the cowboys get their cattle to the eastern cities?_____
_____
_____

3. How many years did cattle drives last? _____

4. Why are there no more cattle drives? _____
_____
_____
_____

Activities:

1. Draw a picture of what you think a cattle drive looked like.

2. Compose a 4-line song that a cowboy might sing while on a cattle
   drive. _____
_____
_____

3. Color your worksheet.

1861-65....
Civil War

CONFEDERACY: 1861-1865

Texas withdrew from the United States to join with 12 other southern states in a war against the northern states. They fought over the right of states to make their own laws, including the decision about slavery. Albert Sidney Johnston and John Hood were famous Texas generals. After the war, Texas became part of the United States again.

#16. <u>1861-65...Civil War</u>

Name _____
_____Date_____
_____

Questions:

1. Why did we have the Civil War? _____
_____
_____
_____
_____
_____
_____
_____

2. How long did the Civil War last? _____
_____

3. Name two Texas generals. _____
_____

4. How many southern states withdrew from the United States
during the Civil War?_____
_____

5. What year did Texas again become a part of the United States?
_____

Activities:
1. Draw and color the six flags that have flown over Texas.

2. Color your worksheet.

1876... Last Indian Battles

UNITED STATES OF AMERICA
1846-1861; 1865

Trying to save their hunting grounds and homes, Indians fought against the white settlers. Quanah Parker, the last great Comanche chief, led the final battles fought by Indians.

#17. <u>Last Indian Battles</u>

Questions:

1. Give a reason why the Indians fought against the white settlers.

_____
_____
_____
_____
_____

2. Who was the last great Comanche chief? _____
_____

3. What do you think happened to all of the Indians after the last battles were fought? _____

_____
_____
_____
_____
_____
_____
_____
_____
_____

Activities:

1. The Plains Indians lived in tepees. Using colored paper and Indian designs, construct your own tepee.

2. Color your worksheet.

Late 1800s... Products

UNITED STATES OF AMERICA
1846-1861; 1865

Barbed wire, citrus fruits, wheat, cotton, cattle, watermelon, and many other products brought prosperity to Texas in the late 1800s.

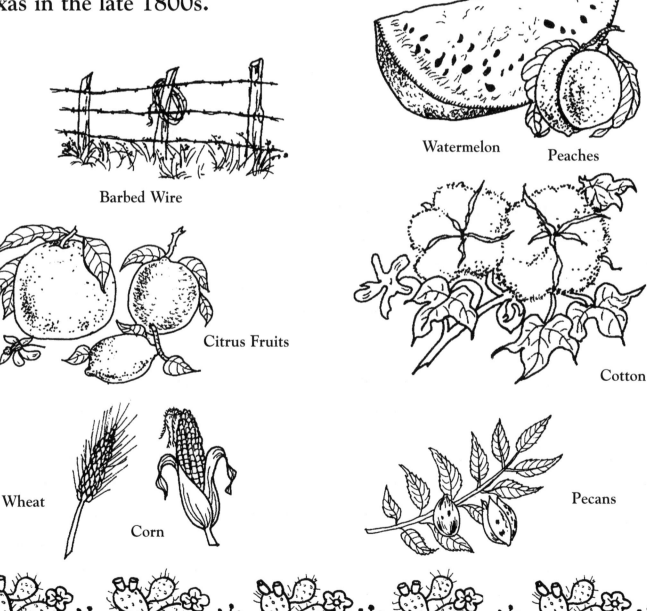

Barbed Wire

Watermelon   Peaches

Citrus Fruits

Cotton

Wheat   Corn   Pecans

18

#18. Late 1800s...Products

Name _____

_____Date_____

_____

Questions:

1. Name 5 products grown in Texas after the Civil War. _____
_____
_____
_____

2. What is barbed wire? _____
_____
_____
_____

   Give a reason for its use. _____
_____

Activities:

1. List all the products shown on your worksheet. _____
_____
_____
_____
_____
_____

2. Put these 10 products shown in alphabetical order. _____
_____
_____
_____
_____

3. Choose one product from the list and tell how it can be used. _____
_____
_____
_____

4. Color your worksheet.

1880s...
State Institutions

State schools and hospitals were built in the 1800s. Prairie View College for black students was opened in 1879.

In 1883, the University of Texas was founded. Near its campus, the red granite state capitol was dedicated in 1888.

#19 1880s...State Institutions

Name _____

_____ Date _____

_____

Questions:

1. a) In what year was Prairie View College founded? _____

   b) In what year was the University of Texas founded? _____

2. The state capitol was dedicated in what year? _____

3. Our state capitol was made of what materials? _____
_____

4. What is on top of the capitol? _____
_____

_____

_____

Activities:

1. Draw and color the two flags shown on the state capitol.

2. Color your worksheet.

1900s...
Industries

UNITED STATES OF AMERICA

The invention of cars, planes, trains, and factory machinery brought a need for oil. In Texas, oil was discovered in great quantity in 1901. People flocked into Texas and cities sprang up overnight.

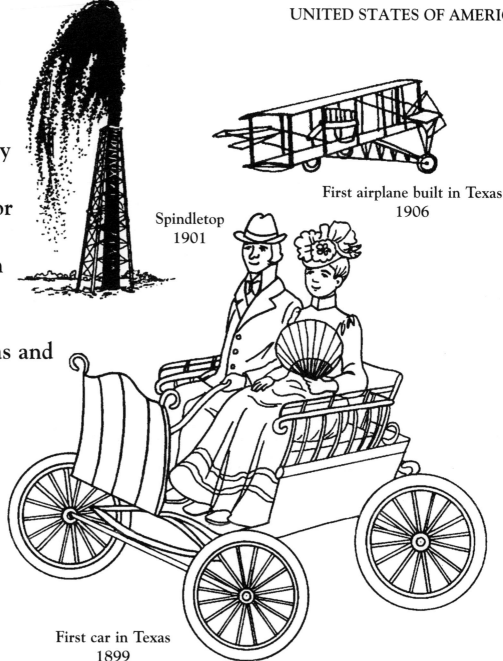

Spindletop
1901

First airplane built in Texas
1906

First car in Texas
1899

#20. <u>1900s...Industries</u>

Questions:

1. Using a dictionary, or a reference book, find the meaning of spindletop. _____
   _____
   _____

2. Of the inventions from the early 1900s, which are still important today? _____
   _____
   _____
   _____

3. Why was the discovery of oil so important? List 5 uses of oil. _____
   _____
   _____
   _____
   _____

4. What caused so many people to come to Texas in the early 1900s?
   _____
   _____
   _____

Activities:

1. Choose the early car or the early airplane and compare it to a modern one. Either write your description or draw your comparison.

2. Color your worksheet.

1914-1918
World War I

UNITED STATES OF AMERICA

More than 200,000 Texans served in a war fought against Germany and its allies. The Battleship Texas was built and took part in many battles. It also served in World War II.

#21. <u>1914-1918...World War I</u>

Questions:

1. Can you name the branches of service shown by the three people in the picture?_____
_____

2. What does it mean to be an "ally" of a country? _____
_____
_____
_____

3. If you were joining a branch of the service for the United States, which one would you choose?_____
Give a reason for your answer._____
_____
_____

Activities:

1. Draw your own battleship.
   Label the parts.

2. Design a new uniform for one of the service persons shown on your worksheet.

3. Color your worksheet.

1920...
Some "Firsts"

UNITED STATES OF AMERICA

The first woman to be elected as governor of Texas was Miriam Ferguson in 1925. The radio, a new invention, became popular and so did the music of "jazz." Airline travel had its beginnings in the city of Dallas.

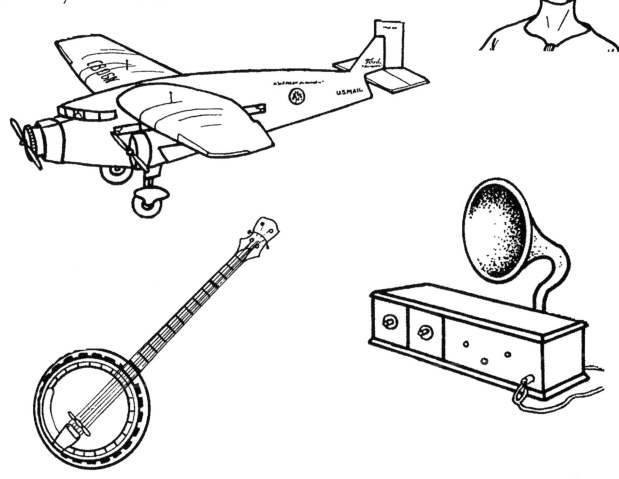

#22. <u>1920...Some "Firsts"</u>

Name _____

_____Date_____

_____

Questions:

1. Has Texas had another woman governor besides Miriam Ferguson? If so, name her. _____
_____

2. What kind of musical instrument is shown on your worksheet?_____
_____

   List two ways it is the same as the piano and two ways it is different. _____
_____
_____
_____

3. How does this airplane differ from the one built in 1906? _____
_____
_____
_____

Activities:

1. Can you compare the form of music called "jazz" to another form of music?_____
_____
_____
_____

2. Compose one verse of your own song._____
_____
_____
_____

3. Color your worksheet.

1929...
Great Depression

UNITED STATES OF AMERICA

All states suffered during the GREAT
DEPRESSION. For 10 years, many people
had no jobs, and both food and
money were scarce. Lack of
rain for several years caused
"Dust Bowls" where no
crops could grow. Finally, by
1937, large dams were
built to help
distribute water
in the state.

#23. 1929...Great Depression

Questions:

1. What is meant by the "Great Depression"? _____

_____

_____

2. What caused the "Dust Bowl"? _____

_____

_____

3. When you look at this picture, can you tell how life was during the
   Great Depression? _____

_____

_____

_____

4. Why did dams help distribute water in the state? _____

_____

_____

_____

Activities:

1. Using a reference book,
   find an illustration of a dam.
   Draw your own diagram of a dam.

2. a) Name one dam in the Austin area. _____

_____

   b) On which river is this dam located? _____

_____

3. Color your worksheet.

1940s...
Arts, Athletics

As the economy grew, everyone had more time to pursue enjoyment of the arts and athletics. Many Texans excelled with their talents and became known throughout the world.

UNITED STATES OF AMERICA

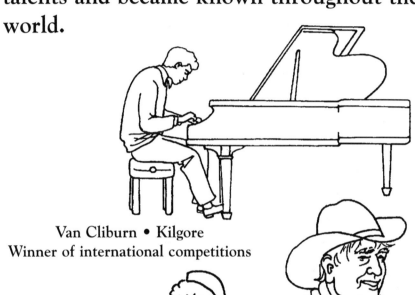

Van Cliburn • Kilgore
Winner of international competitions

Alan Lomax • Austin
Folk music scholar

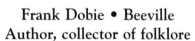

Frank Dobie • Beeville
Author, collector of folklore

Mary Martin • Weatherford
Award-winning actress

Sammy Baugh
Temple
Pro football player

Mildred "Babe" Didrikson • Port Arthur
All-around woman athlete

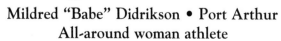

Name _____

Date _____

Questions:

1. Give one example that shows how each of these six Texans on your worksheet is famous. (Use a Texas Almanac or reference book to find your answers). _____

_____

_____

_____

_____

_____

_____

_____

_____

_____

_____

_____

_____

2. If you could be one of these people, which one would you choose and give a reason for your choice. _____

_____

_____

_____

_____

_____

_____

_____

_____

_____

_____

_____

_____

_____

_____

Activities:

1. Color your worksheet.

1941-45
World War II

UNITED STATES OF AMERICA

The United States joined with Allies to win a war against Germany and Japan. Many Texans served in the Armed Forces. General Dwight D. Eisenhower was commander in chief of all Allied Forces. Admiral Chester Nimitz commanded the Naval Forces in the Pacific Ocean. Oveta Culp Hobby was commander of the Women's Auxiliary Corps.

Chester Nimitz
Fredericksburg

Dwight D. Eisenhower
Denison

Oveta Culp Hobby
Houston

Aircraft Carrier

Randolph Field
San Antonio

#25. <u>1941-45...World War II</u>

Questions:

1. What caused the United States to enter World War II? (Use a reference book to find your answer.) _____
_____
_____
_____
_____
_____
_____
_____
_____
_____
_____
_____
_____

2. How long did World War II last?_____

3. Can you name the general who was in charge of all Allied Forces?
_____

Activities:

1. Color your worksheet.

1953-1963... Presidents

UNITED STATES OF AMERICA

Dwight D. Eisenhower was the 34th president of the USA. He served from 1953 to 1961.

Lyndon B. Johnson was president of the USA from 1963 to 1969.

Dwight D. Eisenhower • Denison

Presidential Seal

Lyndon B. Johnson • Stonewall

#26. <u>1953-63...Presidents</u>

Questions:

1. How long did Dwight Eisenhower serve as president of the
   United States? _____

2. How long did Lyndon Johnson serve as president of the
   United States? _____

Activities:

1. Compare the Texas seal to the presidential seal. Tell two ways they
are alike and two ways they are different. _____
_____
_____
_____
_____
_____
_____
_____
_____
_____
_____
_____
_____
_____
_____
_____
_____
_____
_____

2. Color your worksheet.

1963... Integration

UNITED STATES OF AMERICA

An important change was made in Texas when the U.S. government enacted new laws. The laws were made to assure that black people and members of all races would be given equal opportunities in education, jobs, and in all of society. Black men and women as well as members of other cultures came to prominence in the life of Texas.

J. Mason Brewer
Historian and folklorist

Barbara Jordan
Texas Senator 1966-1972
U.S. congresswoman 1972-1978

Porfirio Salinas • El Paso
Painter of Texas scenes

#27. <u>1963...Integration</u>

Name _____
_____Date_____
_____

Questions:

1. What is meant by integration? _____
_____
_____
_____
_____
_____

2. If Texas is a state that is integrated, what does that mean? _____
_____
_____
_____

Activities:
1. Choose one:
   a) Pretend you are J. Mason Brewer. Write your own brief folktale.
   b) Pretend you are Barbara Jordan. Write a new law that you think we should have.
   c) Pretend you are Porfirio Salinas. Draw and color a Texas landscape.

2. Color your worksheet.

1969...
Space Age Begins

UNITED STATES OF AMERICA

NASA
National Aeronautics and
Space Administration

Much of the preparation
and training for
flights into outer space
took place at the
Johnson Space
Center near
Houston.

UNITED STATES

Astronaut Neal Armstrong landing
on the moon July 20, 1969
Apollo 11

#28. <u>1969...Space Age Begins</u>

Name _____
_____Date_____
_____

Questions:

1. When was the first United States flag "planted" on the moon?

_____

   Who had this honor?_____

2. What does NASA stand for? _____

_____

Activities:

1. List some items you would need for your trip to outer space. _____

_____
_____
_____
_____
_____
_____
_____
_____
_____
_____

2. Tell the activities you would be involved in with setting up a space
   station. _____

_____
_____
_____
_____
_____
_____
_____
_____

3. Color your worksheet.

1980s-90s Technology

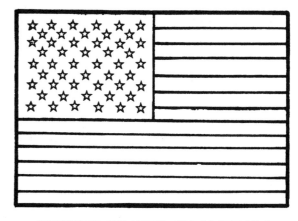

UNITED STATES OF AMERICA

Texas companies played a large part in developing the computer and other technologies. Instant information became available throughout the world and from outer space. As countries of the world become more closely related and interdependent, Texas is working to keep the environment clean and safe for plants, animals, and all living creatures.

#29. <u>1980s-90s...Technology</u>

Name _____

_____Date_____

_____

Questions:

1. How is the world receiving better and quicker information? _____
_____
_____
_____
_____

2. Do you think computers can be used to help keep the environment
safe and clean?_____
_____
_____
_____
_____

3. How would you dispose of your old or outdated computer? _____
_____
_____
_____

Activities:

1. List 4 ways the computer can help you with your schoolwork._____
_____
_____
_____
_____
_____
_____

2. List 3 computer companies. _____
_____
_____
_____

3. Color your worksheet.

2000... a New Century

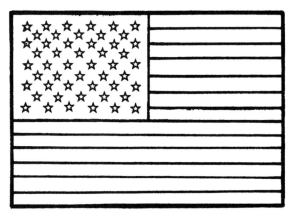

UNITED STATES OF AMERICA

What are some of the things
YOU think will happen in
Texas during the new century?
Family flights to the moon?
Video telephones? Cars that fly?
Plastic "money"? Computer
farming? Texas taco shops on
the moon?
Draw pictures of your ideas.

#30. 2000...A New Century

Name _____

_____ Date _____

_____

_____
_____
_____
_____
_____
_____
_____
_____
_____
_____

_____
_____
_____